Learning Unlimited®

let's play RECORDER

LEVEL TWO

"For Dora"

I0809283

HAL•LEONARD® CORPORATION

7777 W. BLUEMOUND RD. P.O. BOX 13819 MILWAUKEE, WI 53213

introduction

In **Let's Play Recorder** Level One, you learned many of the basics of recorder playing. Level Two moves you on to higher notes, the very low notes, more sharps and flats, new rhythms, and more.

In addition to instruction and exercises, Level Two provides you with plenty of opportunity to apply what you learn by playing dozens of your favorite songs, arranged as solos, duets and ensembles. You'll find songs to play all year 'round - from Thanksgiving to Graduation; from new Year's Day to Mother's Day. And as you play and learn, the whole world of music opens before you.

Ready? Let's play recorder!

does your recorder use... German fingering, or Baroque fingering?

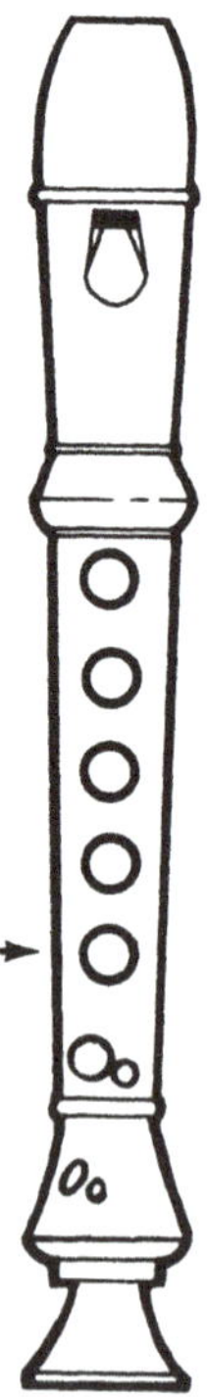

here's one way to tell:

If this hole (the E hole) is **larger** than the one above it, the fingering is Baroque.

If it is **smaller** than the hole above it, the fingering is German.

Which recorder do you have?
BE SURE TO USE THE CORRECT FINGERING

a new note...high E

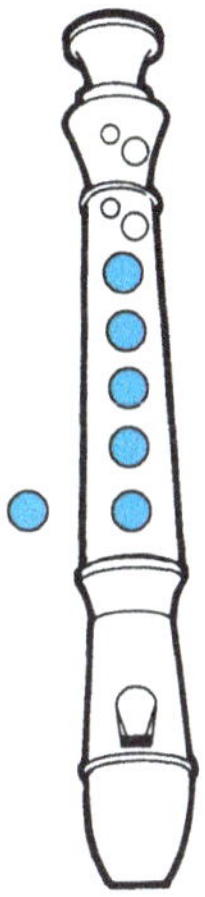

HIGH E

- High E is fingered the same as low E, except for the thumb hole — now called the **octave** hole.

  The fingering diagram shows that the octave hole is half open: ◓

- To open the octave hole correctly:
  1) Keep the thumb firmly against the recorder,
  2) Roll the thumb slowly down until the thumbnail marks the middle of the octave hole.

- High notes require more breath support than lower ones.

Go from low E — played softly, with steady breath support — to high E and back again. Do it in one breath, **legato,** increasing your breath support as you prepare for the high note. Roll the thumb slowly down and back up.

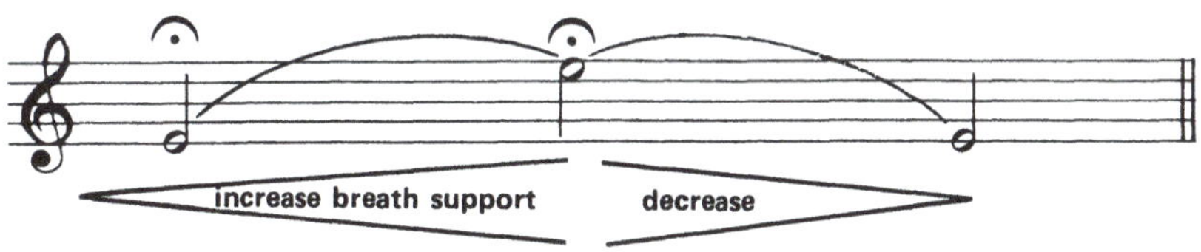

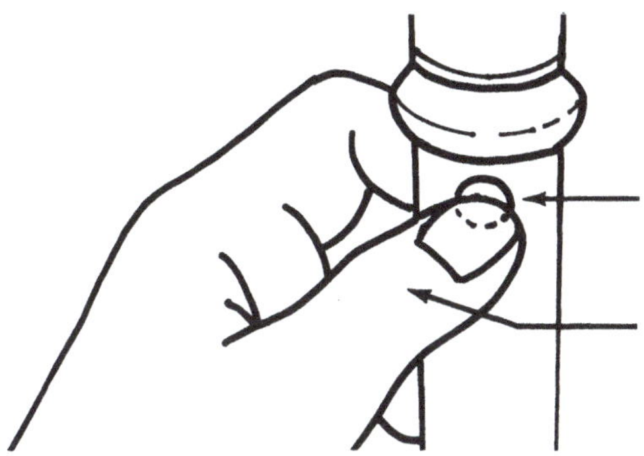

The thumbnail marks the middle of the octave hole.

This knuckle will raise slightly as you roll the thumb down.

DO NOT lift the thumb off the recorder to open the octave hole.

practicing high E

1

Play this exercise slowly, with a steady rhythm, until the thumb moves smoothly from E to E. Watch the phrase markings, and remember to support the high E with more breath.

2

The articulation (attack) of each note must be clear. A **gentle** "too" (or "doo") is as important for high notes as it is in the low register.

3

This exercise, which is an arpeggiated (broken) E minor chord, requires that you prepare to roll the thumb between B and E.

4

In this exercise high E is approached from various notes. Watch the "legato" phrase markings.

America

Words by Samuel Francis Smith
Music by Henry Carey

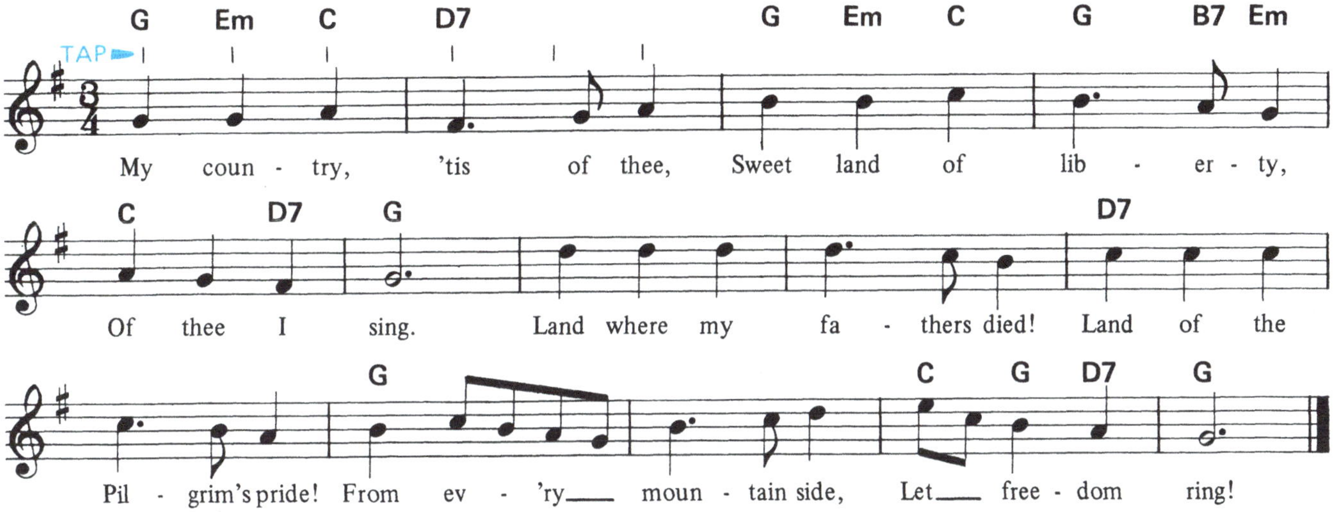

When Johnny Comes Marching Home

The addition of a snare drum or other percussion instruments will enhance the performance of this song.

Louis Lambert

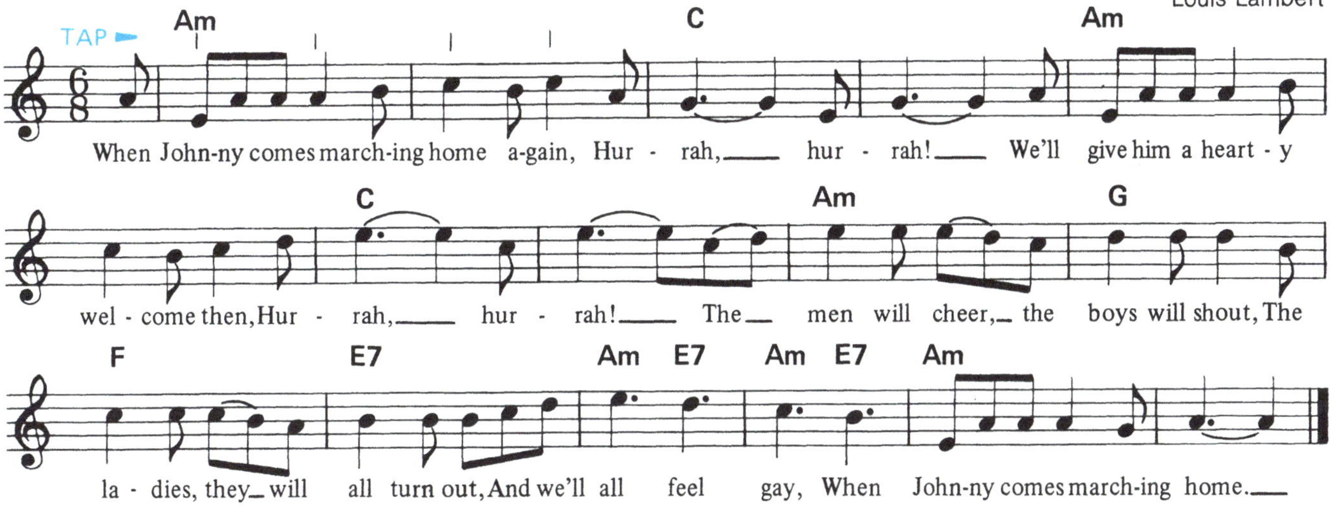

sixteenth notes

You already know that eighth notes are half as long as quarter notes; so two eighth notes are played to one beat. (See Book One, p. 18.)

Sixteenth notes, with two beams, are **one fourth** as long as quarter notes; so **four** sixteenth notes are played to one beat. It's as if you were saying two "jingles" in the time it took to say one.

dotted eighth notes

As you know, a dot after a note increases its time value by one half.

A dotted eighth note is one half longer than an eighth note without a dot — and the note following it becomes one half shorter: a sixteenth note.

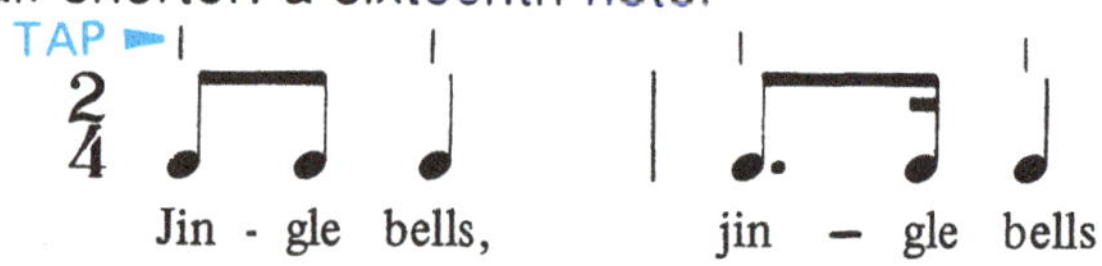

Do you feel the difference?

The following examples make the exact rhythm of the dotted eighth and sixteenth notes clear. Clap each of them.

Jingle Bels

for Melody with Harmony

This song uses:

Battle Hymn Of The Republic
for
Melody with Descant

Pay careful attention to the ♩. ♪ rhythm in the melody. Keep the tempo slow and steady, beginning softly and gradually getting louder.

Words by Julia Ward Howe
Music by William Steffe

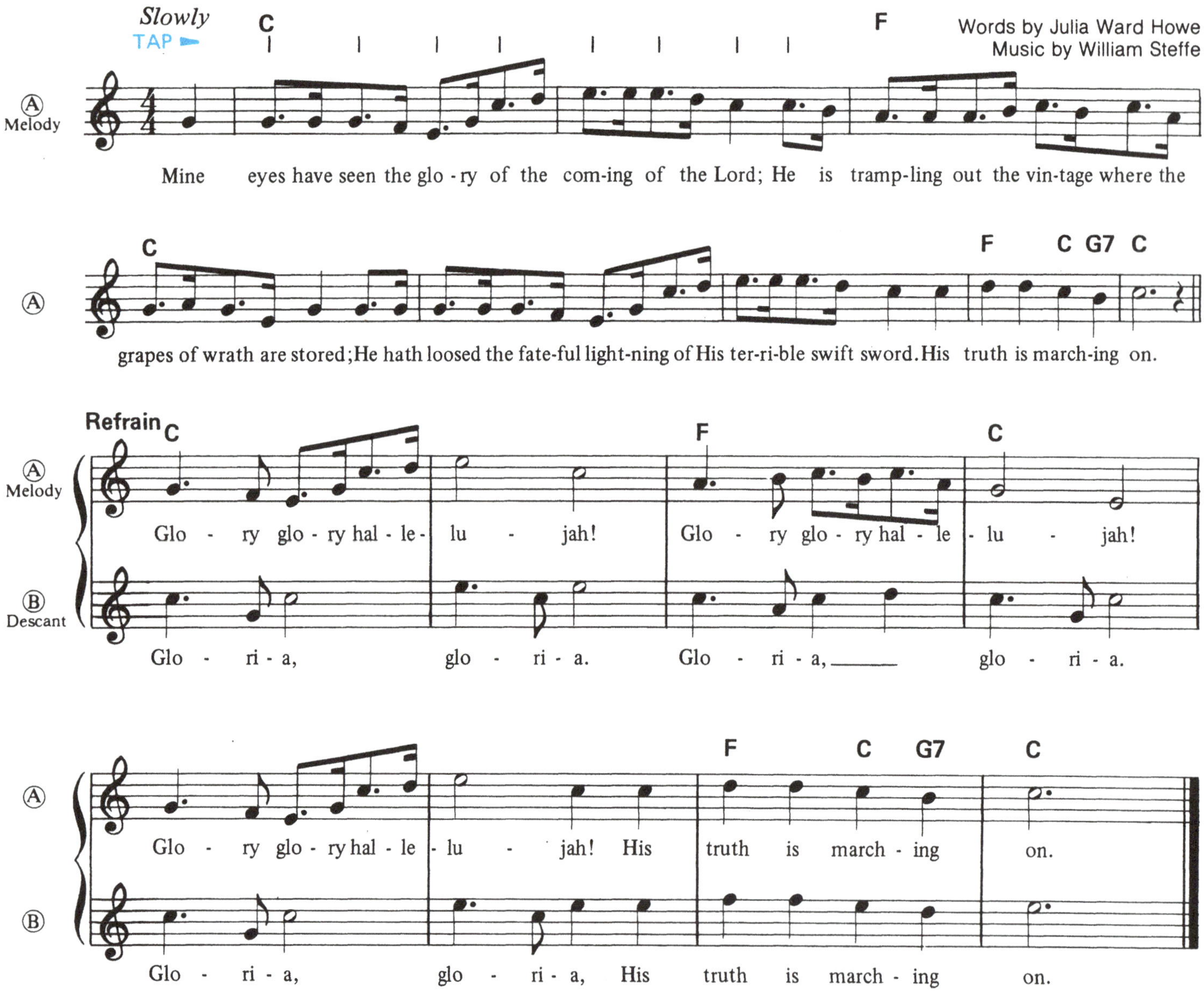

Kum Ba Yah
for Melody with Harmony

The melody should be phrased as a short statement followed by an answer.

African Folk Song

learning high notes...from their low notes

Some notes are fingered **completely differently** from their counterparts an octave lower. You already know some of these:

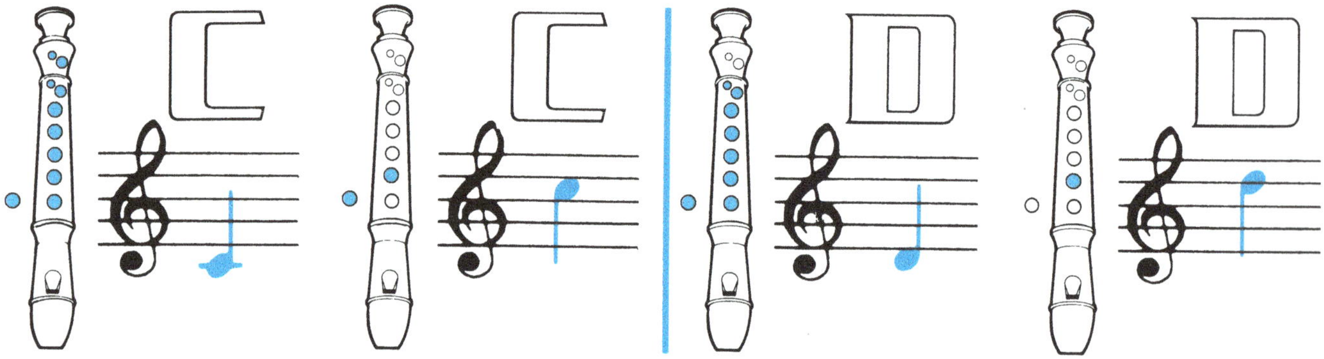

Some notes are fingered the **same** as those an octave below, except in the use of the octave hole. These include high E, which you've just learned, and a new note: high G.

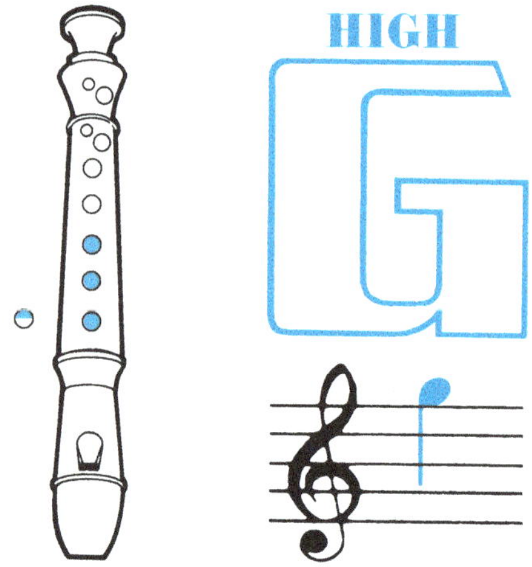

practicing high G

1

2

Other high notes differ only slightly from their low notes. These include high F and high F♯/G♭.

Compare the Baroque fingerings for low F and high F. (The German fingerings for low F and high F are the same except for the octave hole.)

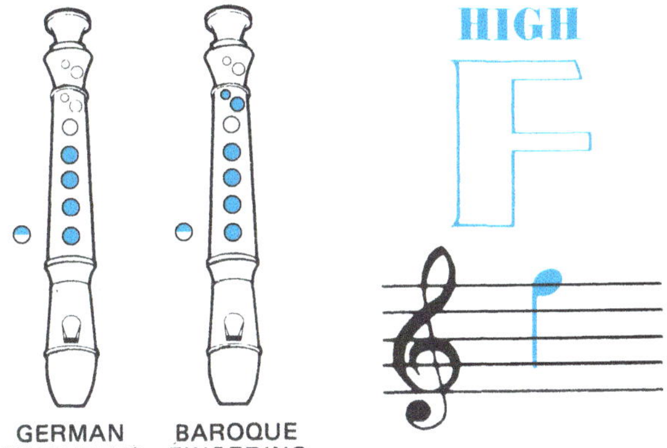

GERMAN FINGERING   BAROQUE FINGERING

practice

Compare the fingerings for low F♯/G♭ and high F♯/G♭.

GERMAN FINGERING   BAROQUE FINGERING

practice

scales using new notes

F major scale

G major scale

finger breakers

Special problems in the F major scale:

1

2

Special problems in the G major scale:

B (ALTERNATE FINGERING)

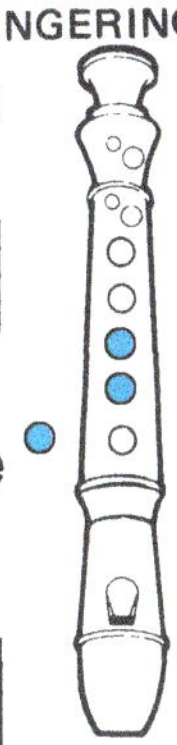

3

An alternate fingering for B will make finger breakers like number 3 easier.

4

Amazing Grace
for
Melody with Harmony

Words by John Newton
Traditional Melody

Over The River And Through The Woods
for Melody with Harmony

Words by Lydia Maria Child
Composer Unknown

Pomp And Circumstance
for
Melody with Harmony and Piano

Use the alternate B fingering (see page 11) in passages like: 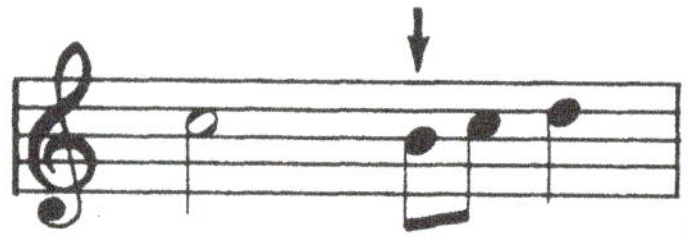

Stately march

Edward Elgar

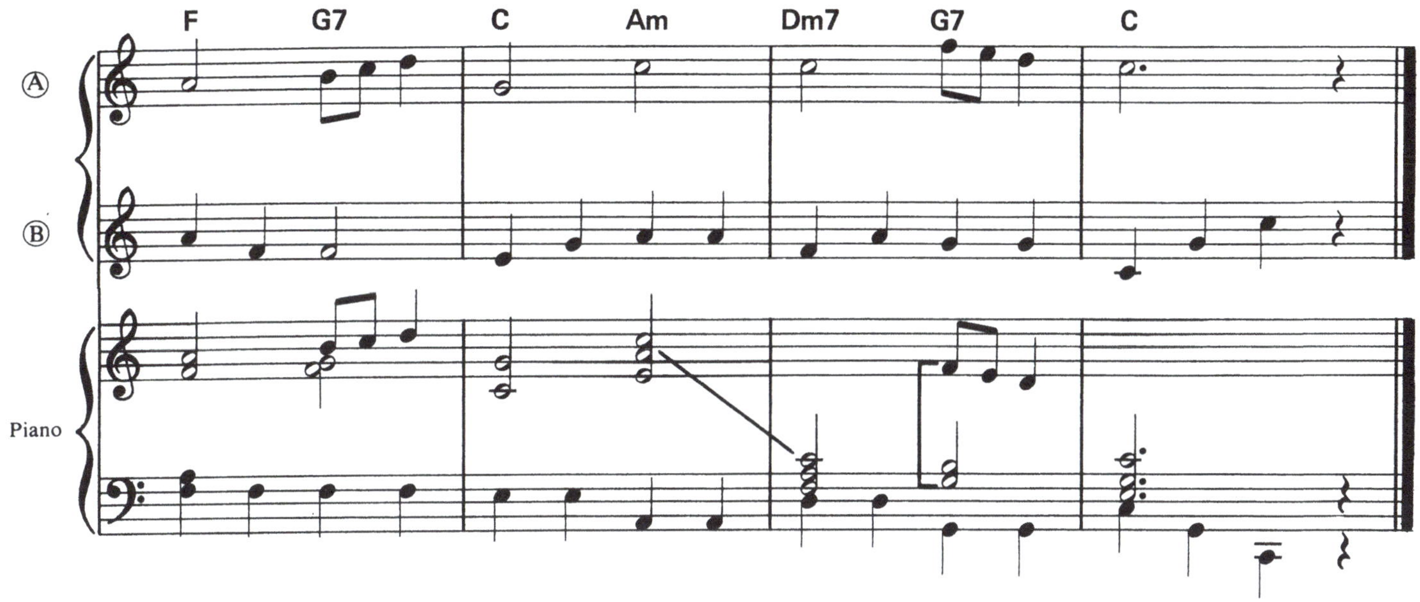

Silent Night
for Melody with Harmony

Words by Joseph Möhr
Music by Franz Grüber

If I Had A Hammer
(The Hammer Song)

Words and Music by
Lee Hays and Pete Seeger

We Gather Together

Netherland Folk Song

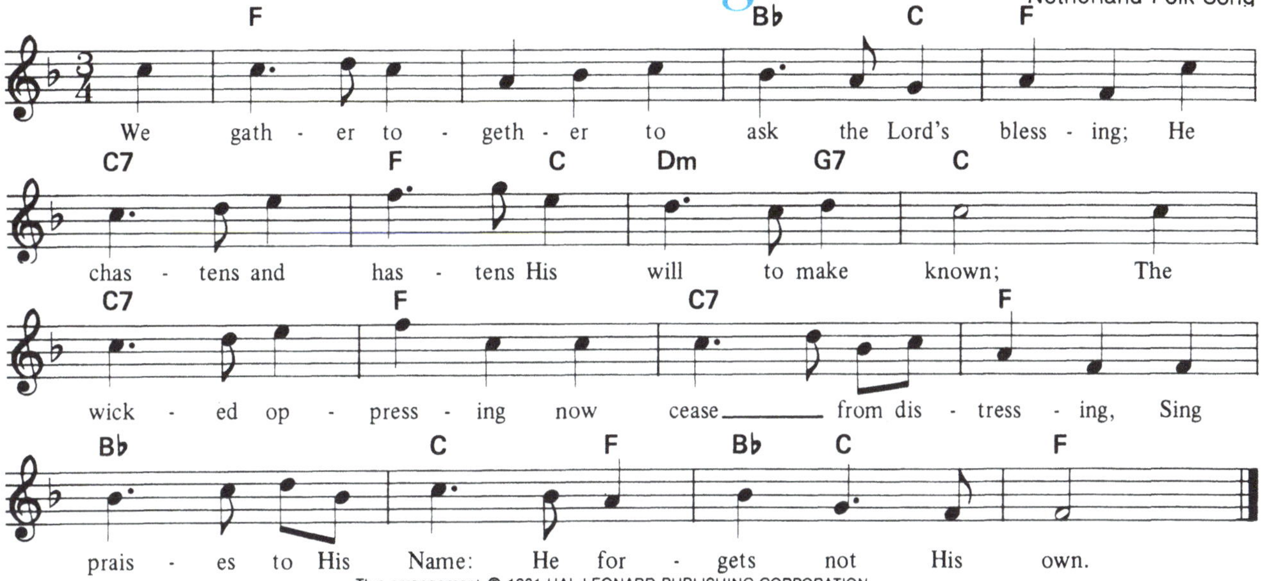

Freedom Of Elections

(Tune: Yankee Doodle)

Traditional

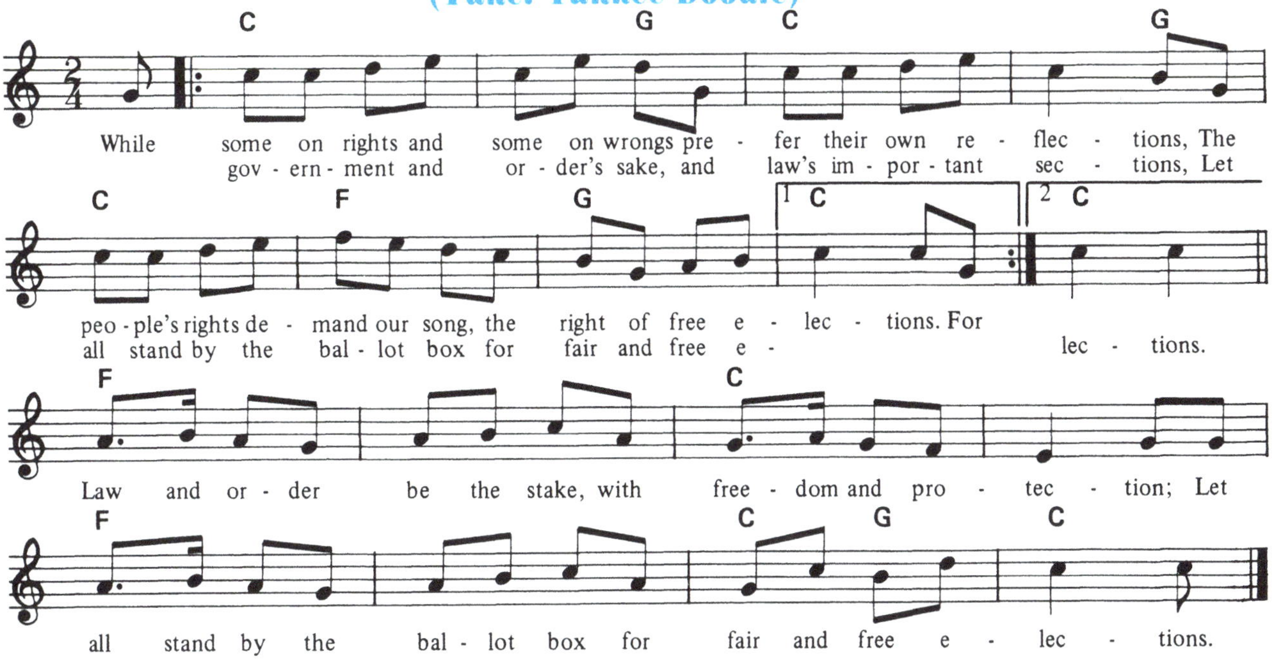

This Land Is Your Land
for Melody with Harmony

Words and Music by
Woody Guthrie

Los Tres Santos Reyes
for
Melody with Harmony

In order to get the "feel" of the syncopated rhythm practice it without the tie:
When you are confident of the placement of the sixteenth note, re-introduce the tie.

The use of maracas, conga, timbales and other percussion instruments will enhance the performance.

a new note...low G♯/A♭

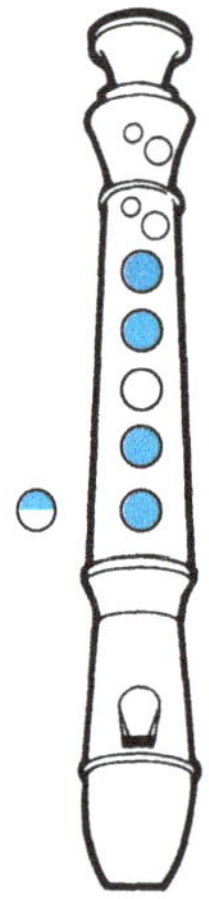

LOW G♯/A♭

Greensleeves

Slowly Traditional

Chiapanecas
for Melody with Harmony

Moderately

Mexican Folk Song

Birthday And Anniversary Song
for
Melody with Harmony

Traditional

Havah Nagilah
for
Melody with Harmony

If percussion is used, the rhythm pattern should be

Israeli Folk Song

Dm
ha - vah n' - ra - n' - na, Ha - vah n'-ra - n' - na
1 E
V' - nis m' - cha,
2 E
V' - nis m' - cha.
Am
U - ru u - ru - a - chim
U-ru - a-chim b'-lev sa-me-ach, U-ru - a-chim b'-lev sa-me-ach,
Dm
U-ru - a-chim b'-lev sa-me-ach,
U-ru - a-chim b'-lev sa-me-ach,
E
U-ru - a-chim u-ru - a-chim
Am E Am
b'lev sa-me - ach.
rit.

Mother's Day
for
Melody with Piano Accompaniment

Words by Paula Ober
Music by Leo Sevush

Dm
E7
Am
Car - ing and shar - ing her love.
Piano
Am
Dm
G
C
Day af - ter day, she shows the way,
Piano
F
Dm
E7
Am
That's why I say Hap - py Moth - er's Day.
Piano

The Star-Spangled Banner
for
Melody with Three-part Harmony

The harmony should be played softly, as the low register won't respond well if "pushed".

Line © of the harmony in particular has important moving lines. More players can be used on this part if desired.

Words by Francis Scott Key
Music by John Stafford Smith

Three-part Harmony for The Star-Spangled Banner

the three notes that do not use the octave hole...D, C♯/D♭, and D♯/E♭

you already know

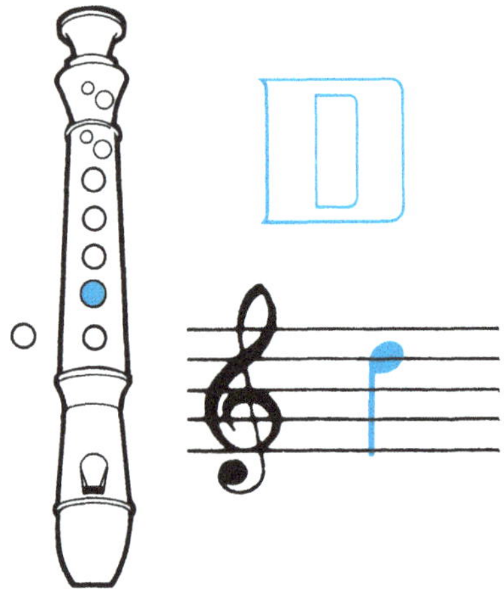

new note:

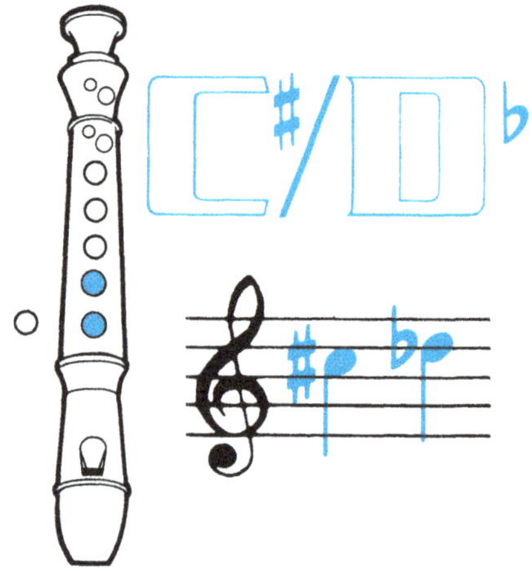

new note:

finger breakers

1 

2 

1 

2 

1 

2 

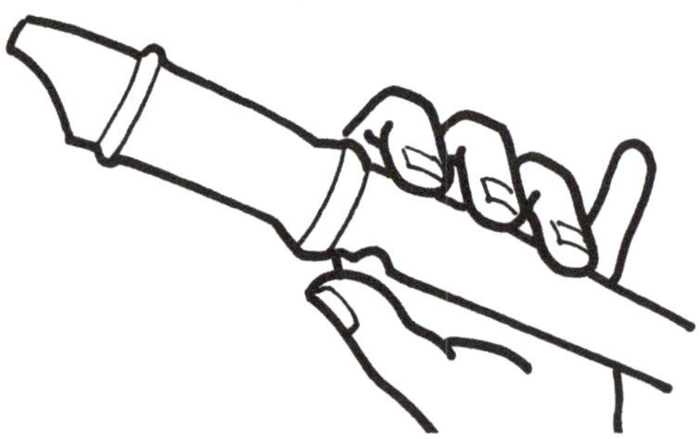

The thumb should move only about a half inch in opening the octave hole, so that it is ready to close it instantly.

triplets

You have learned about:

one note played in one beat  (quarter note)

two notes played in one beat  (eighth notes)

four notes played in one beat  (sixteenth notes)

When **three** notes are played in one beat, they are called a **triplet,** identified by the number 3.

Practice the triplet rhythm using the word "trip-o-let," giving a slight accent to the first syllable of the word.

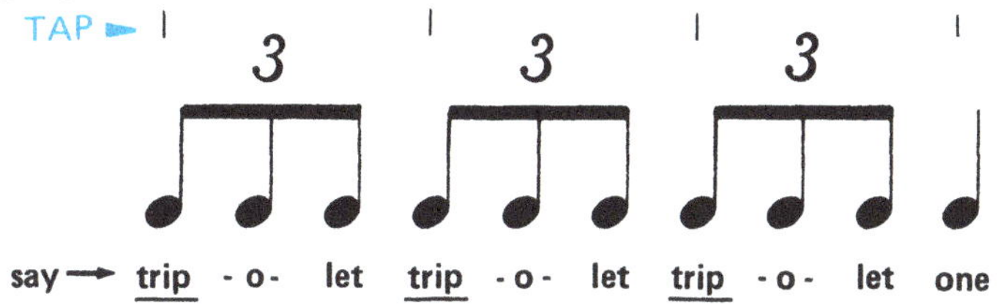

Find the triplets in the song I'VE BEEN WORKING ON THE RAILROAD.

I've Been Working On The Railroad

Traditional

Toreador Song...from Carmen

Georges Bizet

extracting and practicing difficult notes

Each of the circled groups of notes in the Toreador Song is a potential "finger breaker" exercise. Extracting these difficulties and practicing them individually will improve your playing rapidly.

For example, this:

can be practiced like this:

DO THIS WITH DIFFICULTIES IN ALL THE SONGS YOU LEARN.

Consider Yourself
for
Melody with Optional Fill-ins

(From the Columbia Pictures — Romulus film OLIVER!)

The black notes are the melody of the song, while the blue notes are optional fill-ins for more advanced players, which convert the song into a brilliant recorder solo.

Words and Music by
Lionel Bart

F C+ F
Emp - ty lard - er days, why grouse?
Am7 D7
Al - ways a chance we'll meet some - bod - y to foot the bill,
G G♯dim Am A♯dim G7 Dm7
Then the drinks are on the house!
G7 G+7 C G7 C
Con - sid - er your - self our mate,
A7 Dm A+7 Dm
We don't want to have no fuss
B7 C B C B C B C B C Gm
For, aft - er some con - sid - er - a - tion, we can
A7 Dm7
state: Con - sid - er your - self
G7 C
one of us.

double hole notes...low C♯/D♭ and D♯/E♭

The bottom two holes on the recorder are **double holes.**

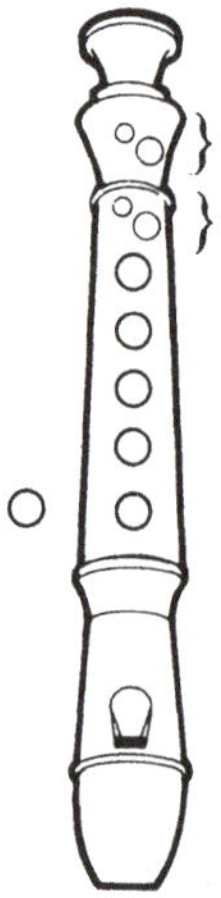

The C hole; when completely covered, the pitch will be C.

The D hole; when completely covered, the pitch will be D.

To raise C or D ½ step to C♯ or D♯, slide the finger back just enough to uncover the smaller hole.

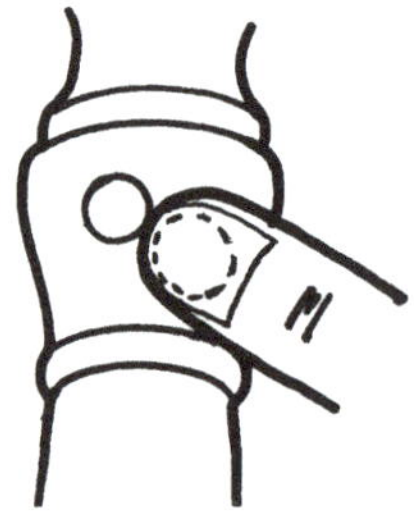

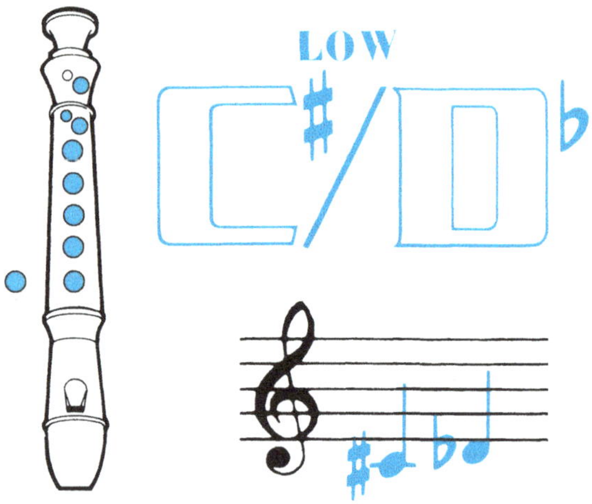

finger breakers

Practice softly and slowly until you can control pitch, tone quality and rhythm.

Chanukah, Oh Chanukah
for
Melody with Harmony

The term "accelerando poco a poco" means to get faster little by little. All repeated notes should be clearly articulated (too-too-too-too), using a light, soft tonguing for speed and clarity.

We Shall Overcome
for Melody with Harmony

New words and music arrangement by Zilphia Horton, Frank Hamilton, Guy Carawan and Pete Seeger

Auld Lang Syne
for Melody with Harmony

Words by Robert Burns
Traditional Melody

new notes...high G♯/A♭ and high A

...high A♯/B♭, B, and C

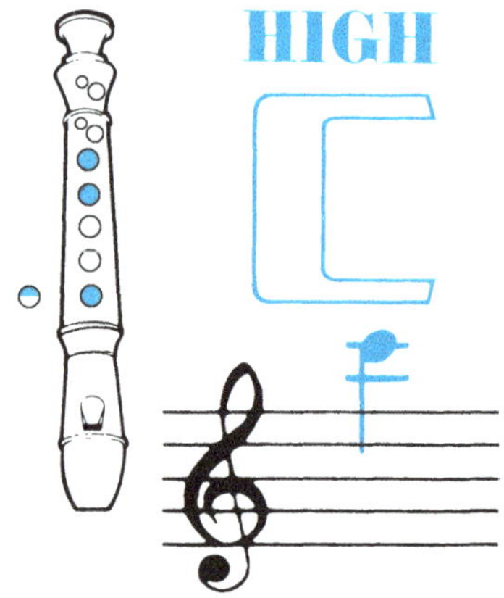

- ✔ The high register, particularly from high G, requires more breath support than the low register.
- ✔ Play each of the high notes, holding for six beats; then play the note again, this time holding for eight beats.
- ✔ Listen for clear tone quality. If necessary, move the mouthpiece and check the octave hole to clear the tone.
- ✔ The high register will become easy after sufficient practice.

developing the high register...
using low register melodies

By playing melodies in the recorder's low octave, then playing them an octave higher, you acquaint yourself with the differences in fingering and breath support between the two registers.

Yankee Doodle

Low register Traditional

High register

Clementine

Low register Traditional

High register

Try this with other low register melodies you've played.

Fingering Chart

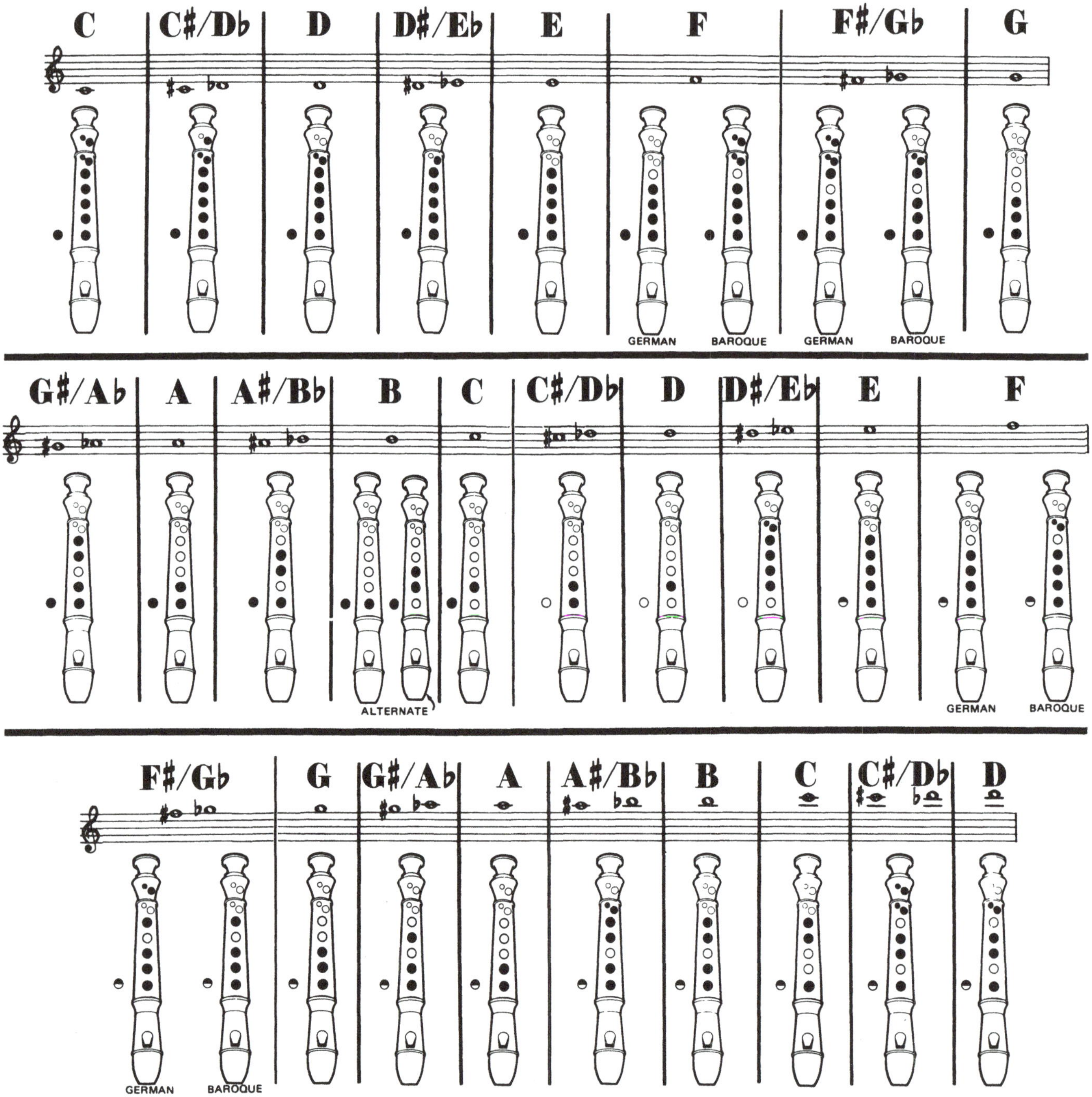